Especially for

_____

From

_____

Date

_____

Happiness Is. . .

Anything Dipped in Chocolate

(AND OTHER SIMPLE PLEASURES)

BARBOUR
PUBLISHING

Published by Barbour Publishing, Inc., P.O. Box 719, Uhrichsville, Ohio 44683, www.barbourbooks.com

Our mission is to publish and distribute inspirational products offering exceptional value and biblical encouragement to the masses.

Printed in China.

Happiness is *anything* dipped in chocolate!

There are four basic food groups:

milk chocolate, dark chocolate,
white chocolate, and chocolate truffles.

What makes life sweet?
Family and friends.
Work and play.
Faith and purpose.
Laughter and tears...
and a little chocolate now and then.

I have this theory that chocolate
slows down the aging process. . . .

*It may not be true,
but do I dare take the chance?*

Strength is the capacity to
break a chocolate bar into four
pieces with your bare hands—
and then eat just one of the pieces.

Judith Viorst

Chocolate Makes the Best Days Even Better

Some of our happiest celebrations throughout the year are made all the more special with a little bit of chocolate. Consider:

- The Valentine's Day box of chocolates

- A wedding reception chocolate fondue fountain

- A fudge-filled chocolate birthday cake

- Fun-size trick-or-treat candy bars

- Chocolate-dipped strawberries for an anniversary

- A holiday cookie-and-candy plate—with enough chocolate to share!

Chocolate really does add a delicious layer of happiness to these events, but it's the memories we store in our hearts and share with family and friends that really make the days worthwhile. And creative chocolate lovers will always find a way to add a little bit of their favorite indulgence to any event!

Chocolate prescription #1:

Bittersweet Chocolate

For unlimited consumption after: long days at work
. . .enduring a child's temper tantrum at the grocery
store. . .calmly handling a roadside emergency. . .

*Looking forward to things
is half the pleasure of them.*

Lucy Maud Montgomery

Chocolate is heavenly, mellow, sensual, deep, dark, sumptuous, gratifying, potent, dense, creamy. . . silky, smooth, luxurious, celestial. Chocolate is. . .happiness, pleasure, love. . . .

ELAINE SHERMAN

Nine out of ten people like chocolate.
The tenth person always lies.

JOHN TULLIUS

I clapped then ate a whole candy bar when
I read a little-known fact about chocolate:
It is derived from cocoa beans,
and beans are vegetables.

TINA KRAUSE

Chocolate lovers know. . .

What's the point of making
chocolate chip cookies if you can't
snag a few chips along the way?

The man is happiest who lives
from day to day and asks no more,
garnering the simple goodness of life.

EURIPIDES

Happiness is. . .
having fantastic friends—
and some really great chocolate!

Chocolate is an experience. . .
one to extend and savor.

Simple pleasures are always
the last refuge of the complex.

OSCAR WILDE

Money may talk, but chocolate sings.

*Happiness does not consist in things,
but in the relish we have of them.*

FRANÇOIS DUC DE LA ROCHEFOUCALD

Inside some of us is a thin person struggling to get out, but they can usually be sedated with a few pieces of chocolate cake.

When life gets sticky,
dip it in chocolate.

CINDY SALZMANN

There's a time for everything:

a time to laugh, a time to cry,
and a time to share a hot fudge
sundae with a girlfriend (or two).

Always serve too much hot fudge
sauce on hot fudge sundaes.
It makes people overjoyed. . . .

JUDITH OLNEY

Those who love, and are unfortunate enough to suffer from the most universal of all gallant illnesses, will find in chocolate the most enlightening consolation.

JEAN-ANTHELME BRILLAT-SAVARIN

I am not overweight—

I am chocolate-enriched!

Lifelong Chocolate Love

How old were you when you discovered your love of chocolate? Maybe you can't remember a time when you weren't a chocolate lover! Sometimes we adults can revisit the comforts of childhood at the bottom of a creamy mug of cocoa (frothy marshmallow moustache and all).

When we discover a fellow chocoholic, we find an instant friend. Who else but a chocophile can understand our delight of trying a new recipe, sharing a unique treat, and finding the sweet contentment of a velvety piece of gourmet chocolate.

Take time today to bless your friends with a chocolate reminder—one of the simple joys of life.

Chocolate prescription #2:

Dark Chocolate

At least one bar after: successfully managing a toddler and a phone call at the same time. . . completing dinnertime, bath-time, story-time, prayer-time, and bedtime before 10 p.m. . .forcing yourself to retire your favorite pair of shoes. . .

Chocolate is cheaper than therapy, and you don't need an appointment.

CATHERINE AITKEN

Nuts just take up the space
where chocolate ought to be.

Chocolate. . . More chocolate. . .
A little more chocolate. . .

Life is good!

*Life is a series
of sweet surprises!*

Every good and perfect gift is from above.

JAMES 1:17 NIV

If you get melted chocolate
all over your hands,
you're eating it too slowly.

Chocolate is not only pleasant of taste,
but it is also a veritable balm for the mouth,
for the maintaining of all glands and humors
in a good state of health. Thus it is, that all
who consume it, possess a sweet breath.

STEPHANI BLANCARDI

God gave the angels wings,
and He gave humans chocolate.

*The best welcome you
could ever wish for? . . .*

A warm smile, open arms, and a chocolate bar.

*It's the little moments
that make life big.*

A few things to cherish: a trusted friend,
a good book, and a secret stash of chocolate.

BONNIE JENSEN

*I never met a
chocolate I didn't like.*

DEANNA TROI

Chocolate is far more than food;
it's a fundamental part of our lives.

THERESA CHEUNG

Life is a smorgasbord—

a little of this and that.
So fill your plate and
don't forget the chocolate!

A certain simplicity of living is
usually necessary to happiness.

HENRY D. CHAPIN

Even on days when your
chocolate cravings go unfulfilled,
every moment is meant to be savored.

Mama always said, "Life is like a box of chocolates. You never know what you're going to get."

FORREST GUMP

I've Never Met a Piece of Chocolate I Didn't Like

Put a bowl of chocolate candy in front of a little kid and she transforms into a vacuum cleaner, sucking up every morsel she can (even if it results in a stomachache). Gourmet or cheap, milk or dark, chocolate is chocolate to a kid. And it's all delicious.

Maybe as an adult you're a little more discerning when it comes to your chocolate. Do yourself a favor and return—even if for just a moment—to a chocolate you enjoyed as a child but have since abandoned for other, more sophisticated tastes. You may unlock some fun memories you had forgotten about!

If you surrender completely to the moments as they pass, you live more richly those moments.

ANNE MORROW LINDBERGH

Each day that passes is filled
with gifts—and chocolates—
for you to unwrap!

Chocolate is the answer.
Who cares what the question is?

I'm going to be happy today. . .
no matter what may come my way.

ELLA WHEELER WILCOX

*A twinkle in the eye
means joy in the heart.*

PROVERBS 15:30 MSG

Whoever is happy will
make others happy, too.

ANNE FRANK

Music expresses love to our ears…
flowers are a visual symbol of our feelings…
and chocolate allows us to taste love's sweetness.

ELLYN SANNA

There are two food groups:
chocolate and fruit.

And if it is fruit, it should be dipped in chocolate.

Man cannot live on chocolate alone. . .

but woman sure can.

My therapist told me the way to achieve
true inner peace is to finish what I start.
So far today, I have finished two bags of M&Ms
and a chocolate cake. I feel better already.

DAVE BARRY

A shared passion for chocolate =
instant friendship!

Chemically speaking, chocolate really
is the world's perfect food.

MICHAEL LEVINE

It has been shown as proof positive
that carefully prepared chocolate is
as healthful a food as it is pleasant;
that it is nourishing and easily digested. . .
that it is above all helpful to people who
must do a great deal of mental work.

Jean-Anthelme Brillat-Savarin

Chocolate prescription #3:

Milk Chocolate

Help yourself to this diluted, over-sweetened type of chocolate if you: break a nail…need some energy but a latte isn't in the budget…handle the third telemarketing call of the evening with grace…

The happiness of life is made up
of minute fractions—the little soon-
forgotten charities of a kiss, a smile,
a kind look, a heartfelt compliment
in the disguise of a playful raillery,
and the countless other infinitesimals
of pleasurable thought and genial feeling.

SAMUEL TAYLOR COLERIDGE

It is not how much we have,
but how much we enjoy,
that makes happiness.

CHARLES SPURGEON

[God] fills my life with good things.

P<small>SALM</small> 103:5 <small>NLT</small>

Shared chocolate
equals twice the joy!

The Togetherness of Chocolate

There's nothing quite like the delectable aromas of a chocolate-something baking in the oven. From chocolate chip cookies to brownies and cakes to fudgy delights, the result of all that work in the kitchen is well worth it (both in the finished product and licking the bowl)!

Consider sharing your love of chocolate baking with other family members—and especially youngsters. Spending time over a mixing bowl may feel a little less like "slaving away in the kitchen" when you share it with people you love. And who knows? If you are a good enough teacher, you may have just found a way to get baked goods without the baking!

*It isn't the great big pleasures
that count the most; it's making
a great deal out of the little ones.*

JEAN WEBSTER

With such a wealth of sensory pleasure in store, no wonder chocolate should be eaten slowly.

CHRISTIAN MCFADDEN AND CHRISTINE FRANCE

Like love, chocolate is sweet and heady, and it nourishes our hearts.

ELLYN SANNA

All you need is love.

But a little chocolate now
and then doesn't hurt.

Charles M. Schulz

Happiness, like chocolate,
was made to be shared.

Giving chocolate to others is an
intimate form of communication,
a sharing of deep, dark secrets.

MILTON ZELMAN

When we share chocolate,
it weaves links between people
on many, many levels.

MICHEL RICHART

Two things that make you feel rich:
faithful friends and dark-chocolate truffles.

BONNIE JENSEN

As I walk through the trials, struggles,
and joys of life. . .the only thing that works
is a little chocolate and a lot of faith.

MIRANDA TOM

If not for chocolate, there would be
no need for control-top pantyhose.
An entire garment industry
would be devastated.

I don't drown my sorrows;
I suffocate them with chocolate.

The feeling of happiness dwells in the soul.

D<small>EMOCRITUS</small>

After a bar of chocolate one can
forgive anybody—even one's relatives.

At the top of the food
chain sits chocolate.

Carefully prepared chocolate is as healthful a food as it is pleasant; it does not cause harmful effects to feminine beauty, but is on the contrary a remedy for them.

JEAN-ANTHELME BRILLAT-SAVARIN

As with most fine things, chocolate has its season. . . .
Any month whose name contains the letter *A*, *E*,
or *U* is the proper time for chocolate.

SANDRA BOYNTON

A Powerful Motivator

What would we do for chocolate? Maybe a better question is: What wouldn't we do for chocolate? Bribe a chocoholic with a delicious morsel of the good stuff, and you might find someone willing to run errands, do laundry, finish a project, clean a room.

Chocolate (in moderation) makes a stressful afternoon at work a little more bearable, bad news a little less dreary.

When it comes down to it, we just can't trust someone who says, "Chocolate? Oh well, I can take it or leave it." (We know who will take it for you. . .they are right over here!)

Chocolate prescription #4:

White Chocolate

Enjoy at your discretion, but beware:
there aren't any cocoa solids in this confection,
so it lacks the emotional healing properties
of real chocolate.

Dip it in chocolate;
it'll be fine.

The cure for almost anything:
a hug and a piece of chocolate.

The small courtesies sweeten life.

CHRISTIAN NESTELL BOVEE

Happiness is life served up with a scoop
of acceptance, a topping of tolerance,
and sprinkles of hope, although
chocolate sprinkles also work.

ROBERT BRAULT